Learn all about Flutter (DART)

Flutter is a cross-platform mobile application development framework created by Google. It is used to develop applications for Android and iOS from a single codebase.

Flutter is a unique framework in that it uses the Dart programming language, which allows for faster development and a more responsive user interface.

The book covers the following:

Chapter 1: Introduction to Flutter and Dart

Overview of Flutter and its advantages

Introduction to the Dart programming language

Setting up the Flutter development environment

Basics of Dart syntax

Flutter architecture and widget hierarchy

Chapter 2: Flutter Widgets

Introduction to Flutter widgets and their role

Working with basic Flutter widgets (Text, Image, Container, etc.)

Layout widgets and organizing the UI (Row, Column, Stack, etc.) in Flutter

Input and interaction widgets (Button, TextField, GestureDetector, etc.) in Flutter

Material Design and Cupertino widgets in Flutter

Chapter 3: State Management in Flutter

Understanding the concept of state in Flutter

Managing state using StatefulWidget and StatelessWidget in Flutter

Local state management techniques (setState, InheritedWidget) in Flutter

Using state management libraries (Provider, Riverpod, MobX) in Flutter

Architectural patterns for state management (BLoC, Redux) in Flutter

Chapter 4: Navigation and Routing in Flutter

Introduction to navigation in Flutter

Navigating between screens and passing data in Flutter

Named routes and route parameters in Flutter

Nested navigation and bottom navigation bars in Flutter

Deep linking and handling app links in Flutter

Chapter 5: Networking and Data Fetching in Flutter

Making HTTP requests with Dart

Fetching and displaying data from APIs in Flutter

Working with RESTful services and JSON data in Flutter

Authentication and secure communication in Flutter

Using libraries for networking (Dio, http, Chopper) in Flutter

Chapter 6: Data Persistence and Storage in Flutter

Introduction to data persistence in Flutter

Working with local databases (Sqflite, Moor) in Flutter

Storing data in key-value pairs (SharedPreferences) in Flutter

File storage and working with images in Flutter

Using cloud-based storage (Firebase Cloud Storage) in Flutter

Chapter 7: Working with External APIs and Services in Flutter

Integrating Firebase services (Authentication, Firestore, Cloud Messaging) in Flutter

Using device features (Camera, Location, Sensors) in Flutter

Accessing device contacts and calendar events in Flutter

Push notifications and in-app messaging in Flutter

Using third-party APIs (Maps, Social media, Payment gateways) in Flutter

Chapter 8: Flutter UI Customization and Theming

Customizing widget appearance with properties in Flutter

Using themes for consistent app styling in Flutter

Creating custom themes and styles in Flutter

Working with fonts and typography in Flutter

Animations and transitions in Flutter

Chapter 9: Advanced Flutter Concepts

Flutter's rendering and layout pipeline

Performance optimization techniques in Flutter

Internationalization and localization in Flutter

Accessibility considerations and best practices in Flutter

Testing and debugging Flutter applications

Chapter 10: Flutter and Native Device Features

Integrating Flutter with existing native code (Android and iOS)

Using platform channels for bi-directional communication in Flutter

Accessing device features and sensors in Flutter

Working with native APIs and libraries in Flutter

Building custom Flutter plugins

Chapter 11: Flutter and Web Development

Introduction to Flutter web development

Building responsive web interfaces with Flutter

Navigation and routing in Flutter web

Interacting with web APIs and services in Flutter

Deploying Flutter web applications

Chapter 12: Deploying and Publishing Flutter Apps

Building and generating app bundles and APKs (Android) in Flutter

Archiving and distributing apps on the App Store (iOS)

Creating app icons and launch screens for Flutter Apps

Testing and debugging Flutter Apps for release

Publishing Flutter apps to Google Play Store and App Store

Chapter 1: Introduction to Flutter and Dart

I was introduced to Flutter and Dart by a friend who is a software engineer. He showed me how to create a simple app that displayed a list of items. I was amazed at how quickly I was able to create the app and how easy it was to use the Dart programming language.

Since then, I have been using Flutter and Dart to create apps for my own personal use. I have found that the combination of the two is very powerful and allows me to create apps that are both beautiful and functional. I am looking forward to continuing to learn more about Flutter and Dart so that I can create even more amazing apps.

Overview of Flutter and its advantages

Flutter is a cross-platform mobile application development framework created by Google. It is used to develop applications for Android and iOS from a single codebase.

Flutter is a unique framework in that it uses the Dart programming language, which allows for faster development and a more responsive user interface.

Some of the advantages of Flutter include:

- It is easy to learn and use
- It is open source
- It has excellent documentation
- It is backed by Google
- It is fast and responsive
- It has a wide range of widgets

If you're looking to develop cross-platform mobile applications, then Flutter is definitely worth considering.

Introduction to the Dart programming language

The Dart programming language is a powerful tool for creating modern web applications. Dart is easy to learn for beginners and has a wide range of features that make it a great choice for building complex web applications.

Setting up the Flutter development environment

I followed the instructions on the Flutter website to set up my development environment. First, I installed the Flutter SDK and then the Dart SDK. Next, I set up my editor of choice and installed the Flutter and Dart plugins. Finally, I ran the 'flutter doctor' command to verify that everything was set up correctly.

Basics of Dart syntax

Dart is a very powerful and easy to use programming language. It has a very simple syntax that makes it easy to read and write code. Dart is a very Object Oriented language and it supports both static and dynamic typing. Dart is also a very portable language and can run on both the JVM and the JavaScript VM.

Flutter architecture and widget hierarchy

Flutter is a mobile app SDK that allows you to write code once and deploy it to both iOS and Android. Flutter architecture is based on the concept of widgets. Widgets are basically user interface (UI) components that can be reused to build larger and more complex UIs.

The widget hierarchy in Flutter is based on the principle of composition. This means that every widget is a combination of other smaller widgets. For example, a button widget is made up of a number of smaller widgets, such as a text widget and an icon widget.

The benefit of this approach is that it makes it very easy to create complex UIs. You can simply reuse existing widgets to build new ones. This also makes it easy to update your UI as new widgets are added or updated.

One downside of the widget hierarchy is that it can be difficult to understand how everything fits together. However, once you get the hang of it, it's actually quite straightforward.

Chapter 2: Flutter Widgets

Introduction to Flutter widgets and their role

Flutter widgets are the building blocks of a Flutter app. They are used to create the app's user interface. Widgets are like the lego blocks of Flutter. They can be used to create simple or complex user interfaces. There are two types of widgets: StatelessWidget and StatefulWidget.

StatelessWidget are widgets that do not require a state. They are immutable. StatelessWidget are used to create static user interfaces. An example of a StatelessWidget would be a button.

StatefulWidget are widgets that require a state. They are mutable. StatefulWidget are used to create dynamic user interfaces. An example of a StatefulWidget would be a text field.

Widgets are used to create the user interface of a Flutter app. They can be used to create simple or complex user interfaces. There are two types of widgets: StatelessWidget and StatefulWidget.

Working with basic Flutter widgets (Text, Image, Container, etc.)

I was working with some basic Flutter widgets today and I have to say, they are really easy to use! I was able to add a text widget, an image widget, and a container widget with no problem. The text widget was especially easy to use and I was able to format it exactly how I wanted. Overall, I'm really impressed with how easy it is to use these widgets and I'm looking forward to using them more in the future.

Layout widgets and organizing the UI (Row, Column, Stack, etc.) in Flutter

Layout widgets are critical for organizing the UI in Flutter. There are several different layout widgets available, each with its own strengths and weaknesses. The most common layout widgets are Row, Column, and Stack.

Row and Column are both linear layout widgets. Row widgets arrange their children horizontally, while Column widgets arrange their children vertically. Stack widgets are more flexible, allowing children to be arranged in any order.

Each layout widget has its own set of options for controlling the size and position of children. For example, Row and Column widgets both have options for controlling the main axis and cross axis. Stack widgets have options for controlling the stack order and the alignment of children.

Layout widgets are critical for organizing the UI in Flutter. Without them, it would be very difficult to create anything more than a simple list of items. The different layout widgets available give developers a lot of flexibility in how they want to arrange their UI.

Input and interaction widgets (Button, TextField, GestureDetector, etc.) in Flutter

Input and interaction widgets are the backbone of any Flutter app. They allow the user to input information, interact with the app, and provide feedback.

Button is the most basic input widget. It has a text label and an onPressed callback. When the button is pressed, the onPressed callback is called.

TextField is a widget that allows the user to input text. It has a decoration that can be used to customize the look of the text field. It also has an onChanged callback that is called when the text in the text field changes.

GestureDetector is a widget that detects gestures. It has an onTap callback that is called when the widget is tapped. It also has an onDoubleTap callback that is called when the widget is double tapped.

These input and interaction widgets are essential for any Flutter app. They allow the user to input information and interact with the app.

Material Design and Cupertino widgets in Flutter

Flutter provides a set of Material Design widgets. Material Design is an adaptable system—backed by open-source code—that helps teams build high quality digital experiences.

Cupertino widgets implements the current iOS design language based on Apple's Human Interface Guidelines.

Both Material Design and Cupertino widgets are available in the flutter package. To use either set of widgets, import the corresponding package.

```dart
import 'package:flutter/material.dart';

import 'package:flutter/cupertino.dart';
```

If you're creating a mixed app that needs to support both iOS and Android, you can use the CupertinoTheme widget to configure the overall theme of your app to match the current platform.

When using Material Design widgets in Cupertino, be aware that not all Material Design features are available on iOS. In particular, the use of raised buttons is discouraged in Cupertino.

Chapter 3: State Management in Flutter

Understanding the concept of state in Flutter

The state of a widget is information that can be read synchronously when the widget is built and that might change during the lifetime of the widget. It is the responsibility of the widget implementer to ensure that the widget's state is promptly updated when the state changes.

There are two kinds of state in Flutter:

1. Ephemeral state

2. App state

Ephemeral state is also called widget state or UI state. It is the state that exists within the lifetime of a single widget and it is not persisted beyond the lifetime of the widget. Ephemeral state is used to track information that might change during the lifetime of a widget, such as the current selected tab in a TabBar.

App state is also called application state or persisted state. It is the state that exists beyond the lifetime of a single widget and it is persisted in some way, such as in a database. App state is used to track information that needs to be persisted even when the widget is not visible, such as the currently logged in user.

In order to understand the concept of state in Flutter, it is important to understand the difference between these two types of state.

Managing state using StatefulWidget and StatelessWidget in Flutter

When it comes to managing state in a Flutter application, there are two main widget types that you can use: StatefulWidget and StatelessWidget. As the name suggests, a StatefulWidget is a widget that has a state associated with it, whereas a StatelessWidget is a widget that does not have a state associated with it.

If you want to manage state in a Flutter application, then you need to use a StatefulWidget. The reason for this is because a StatefulWidget can be rebuilt whenever the state changes, which means that the widget will always be up-to-date with the latest state. On the other hand, a StatelessWidget will only be rebuilt when the widget is first created, and will not be updated if the state changes.

When it comes to managing state, there are two main approaches that you can take:

1. Use a StatefulWidget and manage the state yourself.

2. Use a StatelessWidget and let the framework manage the state for you.

If you want to have full control over the state of your application, then you need to use a StatefulWidget. This gives you the ability to update the state of your widget whenever you need to, and also allows you to rollback the state if necessary. However, managing state can be a bit tricky, and you need to be careful to not introduce any bugs into your application.

If you want to let the framework manage the state for you, then you can use a StatelessWidget. This is the recommended approach if you don't need to have full control over the state of your application. StatelessWidget s are simpler to use and are less likely to introduce bugs into your application.

Local state management techniques (setState, InheritedWidget) in Flutter

There are two primary techniques for managing state in Flutter: setState and InheritedWidget.

SetState is the most basic state management technique. It simply allows you to update the state of a widget from within the widget itself. This is great for simple state changes, but can quickly become cumbersome for more complex state management.

InheritedWidget is a more advanced state management technique. It allows you to define a widget that can be inherited by other widgets. This allows you to manage state in a more central location, making it easier to update multiple widgets at once.

Both of these techniques have their pros and cons, and it's up to you to decide which one is best for your particular needs.

Using state management libraries (Provider, Riverpod, MobX) in Flutter

The Provider package is a great way to manage state in Flutter. It is easy to use and has a lot of features that make it a great choice for state management.

Riverpod is another state management library that is also easy to use and has a lot of features.

MobX is a state management library that is a bit more complex than Provider and Riverpod but it is very powerful and has a lot of features.

Architectural patterns for state management (BLoC, Redux) in Flutter

The architectural patterns for state management in Flutter are BLoC and Redux.

BLoC stands for Business Logic Component, and it is a pattern that separates business logic from the UI. This separation of concerns makes it easier to test and maintain your code.

Redux is a state management tool that helps you keep your state organized and predictable. It is a good choice for large projects with complex state.

Both of these patterns can be used in Flutter to manage state.

Chapter 4: Navigation and Routing in Flutter

Introduction to navigation in Flutter

In this article, we will be discussing how to implement navigation in Flutter. We will cover the following topics:

1) Creating a basic Flutter application with a Material App.

2) Adding a drawer to our Material App.

3) Adding a floatingActionButton.

4) Adding a BottomNavigationBar.

5) Adding a TabBar.

6) Adding a PageView.

7) Routing to a new page.

8) Returning data from a route.

Creating a basic Flutter application with a Material App:

We will start by creating a new Flutter project. We will name our project "navigation_drawer".

Once our project is created, we will open the main.dart file and replace the default code with the following:

```
import 'package:flutter/material.dart'; void main()
=> runApp(MyApp()); class MyApp extends
StatelessWidget { // This widget is the root of our
application. @override Widget build(BuildContext
context) { return MaterialApp( title: 'Navigation
Drawer', theme: ThemeData( primarySwatch:
Colors.blue, ), home: MyHomePage(), ); } } class
MyHomePage extends StatelessWidget {
@override Widget build(BuildContext context) {
return Scaffold( appBar: AppBar( title:
Text('Navigation Drawer'), ), body: Center( child:
Text('Home Page'), ), ); } }
```

In the code above, we have created a basic Material App with a single Scaffold widget. The Scaffold widget provides us with a default app bar, a body, and a floatingActionButton.

Adding a drawer to our Material App:

We can add a drawer to our Material App by using the Drawer widget. The Drawer widget takes a list of widgets as its children. These widgets will be displayed in the drawer.

We will add the following code to our main.dart file:

```
class MyHomePage extends StatelessWidget {
@override Widget build(BuildContext context) {
return Scaffold( appBar: AppBar( title:
Text('Navigation Drawer'), ), body: Center( child:
Text('Home Page'), ), drawer: Drawer( child:
ListView( children: <Widget>[ DrawerHeader(
child: Text('Drawer Header'), decoration:
BoxDecoration( color: Colors.blue, ), ), ListTile(
title: Text('Item 1'), onTap: () {}, ), ListTile( title:
Text('Item 2'), onTap: () {}, ), ], ), ), ); } }
```

In the code above, we have added a Drawer widget to our Scaffold. The Drawer widget has a header and two ListTiles. The header is optional but we have included it in our example.

Adding a floatingActionButton:

We can add a floatingActionButton to our Material App by using the floatingActionButton property of the Scaffold widget.

We will add the following code to our main.dart file:

```
class MyHomePage extends StatelessWidget {
@override Widget build(BuildContext context) {
return Scaffold( appBar: AppBar( title:
Text('Navigation Drawer'), ), body: Center( child:
Text('Home Page'), ), drawer: Drawer( child:
ListView( children: <Widget>[ DrawerHeader(
child: Text('Drawer Header'), decoration:
BoxDecoration( color: Colors.blue, ), ), ListTile(
title: Text('Item 1'), onTap: () {}, ), ListTile( title:
Text('Item 2'), onTap: () {}, ), ], ), ),
floatingActionButton: FloatingActionButton(
onPressed: () {}, child: Icon(Icons.add), ), ); } }
```

In the code above, we have added a floatingActionButton to our Scaffold. The floatingActionButton is displayed at the bottom right of the screen.

Adding a BottomNavigationBar:

We can add a BottomNavigationBar to our Material App by using the bottomNavigationBar property of the Scaffold widget.

We will add the following code to our main.dart file:

```
class MyHomePage extends StatelessWidget {
@override Widget build(BuildContext context) {
return Scaffold( appBar: AppBar( title:
Text('Navigation Drawer'), ), body: Center( child:
Text('Home Page'), ), drawer: Drawer( child:
ListView( children: <Widget>[ DrawerHeader(
child: Text('Drawer Header'), decoration:
BoxDecoration( color: Colors.blue, ), ), ListTile(
title: Text('Item 1'), onTap: () {}, ), ListTile( title:
Text('Item 2'), onTap: () {}, ), ], ), ),
floatingActionButton: FloatingActionButton(
onPressed: () {}, child: Icon(Icons.add), ),
bottomNavigationBar: BottomNavigationBar(
items: [ BottomNavigationBarItem( icon:
Icon(Icons.home), title: Text('Home') ),
BottomNavigationBarItem( icon:
Icon(Icons.search), title: Text('Search') ),
BottomNavigationBarItem( icon: Icon(Icons.add),
title: Text('Add') ), ], ), ); } }
```

In the code above, we have added a BottomNavigationBar to our Scaffold. The BottomNavigationBar takes a list of BottomNavigationBarItems. Each BottomNavigationBarItem has an icon and a title.

Adding a TabBar:

We can add a TabBar to our Material App by using the tabs property of the AppBar widget.

We will add the following code to our main.dart file:

```
class MyHomePage extends StatelessWidget {
@override Widget build(BuildContext context) {
return Scaffold( appBar: AppBar( title:
Text('Navigation Drawer'), tabs: [ Tab(icon:
Icon(Icons.home), text: 'Home'), Tab(icon:
Icon(Icons.search), text: 'Search'), Tab(icon:
Icon(Icons.add), text: 'Add'), ], ), body: Center(
child: Text('Home Page'), ), drawer: Drawer( child:
ListView( children: <Widget>[ DrawerHeader(
child: Text('Drawer Header'), decoration:
BoxDecoration( color: Colors.blue, ), ), ListTile(
title: Text('Item 1'), onTap: () {}, ), ListTile( title:
Text('Item 2'), onTap: () {}, ), ], ), ), ),
floatingActionButton: FloatingActionButton(
```

```
onPressed: () {}, child: Icon(Icons.add), ),
bottomNavigationBar: BottomNavigationBar(
items: [ BottomNavigationBarItem( icon:
Icon(Icons.home), title: Text('Home') ),
BottomNavigationBarItem( icon:
Icon(Icons.search), title: Text('Search') ),
BottomNavigationBarItem( icon: Icon(Icons.add),
title: Text('Add') ), ], ), ); } }
```

In the code above, we have added a TabBar to our
AppBar. The TabBar takes a list of Tab widgets.
Each Tab has an icon and a text label.

Adding a PageView:

We can add a PageView to our Material App by
using the PageView widget.

We will add the following code to our main.dart
file:

```
class MyHomePage extends StatelessWidget {
@override Widget build(BuildContext context) {
return Scaffold( appBar: AppBar( title:
Text('Navigation Drawer'), ), body: PageView(
children: [ Container( child: Text('Page 1'), ),
Container( child: Text('Page 2'), ), Container( child:
```

```
Text('Page 3'), ), ], ), drawer: Drawer( child:
ListView( children: <Widget>[ DrawerHeader(
child: Text('Drawer Header'), decoration:
BoxDecoration( color: Colors.blue, ), ), ListTile(
title: Text('Item 1'), onTap: () {}, ), ListTile( title:
Text('Item 2'), onTap: () {}, ), ], ), ),
floatingActionButton: FloatingActionButton(
onPressed: () {}, child: Icon(Icons.add), ),
bottomNavigationBar: BottomNavigationBar(
items: [ BottomNavigationBarItem( icon:
Icon(Icons.home), title: Text('Home') ),
BottomNavigationBarItem( icon:
Icon(Icons.search), title: Text('Search') ),
BottomNavigationBarItem( icon: Icon(Icons.add),
title: Text('Add') ), ], ), ); } }
```

In the code above, we have added a PageView to
our Scaffold. The PageView takes a list of widgets
as its children. In our example, we have used three
Container widgets.

Routing to a new page:

We can route to a new page by using the Navigator
widget.

We will add the following code to our main.dart
file:

```
class MyHomePage extends StatelessWidget {
@override Widget build
```

Navigating between screens and passing data in Flutter

In Flutter, there are two main ways to navigate between screens: through the use of Routes or by using the Navigator class.

Routes are static definitions of where a user should go, and they are typically used for pages that do not need to be dynamic, such as an About page. To use Routes, you first need to define them in your MaterialApp widget.

Navigator, on the other hand, is a class that allows for more flexibility and is often used for pages that are more dynamic, such as a user's profile page. With Navigator, you can push and pop pages from a stack, as well as pass data between them.

To pass data between screens, you can use the Navigator's push() method. This method takes two arguments: the first is the Route to which you are pushing, and the second is the data that you want

to pass. The data will be available to the pushed
Route through the ModalRoute.of() method.

Assuming you have two screens, ScreenA and
ScreenB, and you want to pass data from ScreenA
to ScreenB, your code might look something like
this:

```dart
void main() {

runApp(MyApp());

}

class MyApp extends StatelessWidget {

@override

Widget build(BuildContext context) {

return MaterialApp(

title: 'Flutter Demo',

theme: ThemeData(

primarySwatch: Colors.blue,

),

home: ScreenA(),

);
```

```dart
    }
  }
class ScreenA extends StatelessWidget {
  @override
  Widget build(BuildContext context) {
    return Scaffold(
      appBar: AppBar(
        title: Text('Screen A'),
      ),
      body: Center(
        child: RaisedButton(
          child: Text('Push to Screen B'),
          onPressed: () {
            Navigator.push(
              context,
              MaterialPageRoute(
                builder: (context) => ScreenB(),
              ),
```

```dart
      // Pass data to ScreenB here
    );
  },
  ),
  ),
);
}
}
class ScreenB extends StatelessWidget {
@override
Widget build(BuildContext context) {
// Retrieve data from the ModalRoute of the
ScreenA
final data =
ModalRoute.of(context).settings.arguments;
return Scaffold(
appBar: AppBar(
title: Text('Screen B'),
),
```

```
body: Center(

child: Text(data),

),

);

}

}
```

Named routes and route parameters in Flutter

In Flutter, named routes are used to navigate to a specific page, while route parameters are used to pass data to the page that is being navigated to.

For example, let's say we have a page that displays a list of products. We can navigate to this page by using the named route 'products'.

On this page, we can use route parameters to pass in the ID of the product that we want to view. This would be done by using the following URL:

products/123

Where '123' is the ID of the product that we want to view.

When the user navigates to this URL, the 'products' page will be displayed, and the ID of the product will be passed to the page, which can then be used to fetch and display the correct product.

Nested navigation and bottom navigation bars in Flutter

Bottom navigation bars are typically used in conjunction with a top-level navigation bar. In a typical app, there are four or five top-level screens, each with its own set of nested screens. The bottom navigation bar makes it easy to switch between these screens by providing a simple, tabbed interface.

In Flutter, bottom navigation bars are usually used with the Scaffold widget. The Scaffold widget provides a convenient way to create a bottom navigation bar that is attached to a drawer.

To create a bottom navigation bar, you need to use the BottomNavigationBar widget. The

BottomNavigationBar widget takes three arguments:

itemCount: The number of tabs in the bottom navigation bar.

currentIndex: The index of the selected tab.

onTap: A callback that is called when a tab is tapped.

The onTap callback takes an int argument that represents the index of the tapped tab.

In addition to the BottomNavigationBar widget, you also need to use the BottomNavigationBarItem widget. The BottomNavigationBarItem widget is used to represent each tab in the bottom navigation bar. It takes two arguments:

icon: The icon of the tab.

title: The title of the tab.

To create a top-level navigation bar, you can use the AppBar widget. The AppBar widget is typically used with the Scaffold widget. The Scaffold widget provides a convenient way to create a top-level navigation bar that is attached to a drawer.

To create a top-level navigation bar, you need to use the AppBar widget. The AppBar widget takes three arguments:

leading: The widget to display in the left area of the app bar.

title: The widget to display in the center area of the app bar.

actions: The widget to display in the right area of the app bar.

The AppBar widget also has a number of properties that you can use to customize the behavior of the app bar. For example, you can use the automaticallyImplyLeading property to control whether the leading widget is automatically added to the app bar.

In addition to the AppBar widget, you also need to use the Navigator widget. The Navigator widget is used to manage the stack of screens in a Flutter app. The Navigator widget has a number of methods that you can use to push and pop screens from the stack.

To push a new screen onto the stack, you use the push() method. The push() method takes a Route object. The Route object defines the new screen that you want to push onto the stack.

To pop a screen from the stack, you use the pop() method. The pop() method takes an optional argument that represents the result of the popped screen.

The Navigator widget also has a number of properties that you can use to customize the behavior of the navigator. For example, you can use the onPop() property to control what happens when the back button is pressed.

Bottom navigation bars and top-level navigation bars are two of the most important widgets in a

Flutter app. They are used to manage the stack of screens in an app and to provide a simple, tabbed interface for switching between screens.

Deep linking and handling app links in Flutter

Deep linking is the ability to launch a specific screen within an app from another app or from a web page. App links are the standard way to deep link into an Android app. When a user clicks on a deep link, they are taken directly to the content within the app that they are looking for.

Deep links can be used to launch content in an app from a variety of sources, such as:

- Another app

- A web page

- An email

- A social media post

To handle deep links in Flutter, you need to add a few lines of code to your app. First, you need to add a new route to your MaterialApp widget. This route will be used to handle deep links that are launched from outside of your app.

Next, you need to add a method that will be called when your app is launched from a deep link. This method will take the deep link as an argument and navigate to the appropriate screen within your app.

Finally, you need to add a method that will be called when your app is launched from a web page. This method will take the URL of the web page as an argument and navigate to the appropriate screen within your app.

Deep linking can be a great way to make your app more discoverable and to help users navigate to the content they are looking for. By adding a few lines of code, you can make your app more accessible and user-friendly.

Chapter 5: Networking and Data Fetching in Flutter

Making HTTP requests with Dart

Dart provides a great way to make HTTP requests with its built-in HttpClient class. All you need to do is import the dart:io library and you're good to go.

The HttpClient class provides a way to make HTTP requests and receive responses from a server. It also supports streaming data for both request and response. This makes it ideal for use with Flutter, which is a framework for building cross-platform applications.

To make a request, you simply need to create a new HttpClient instance and call the request method. This method takes a URL and returns a Future that will resolve to an HttpClientRequest instance.

Once you have the request, you can add headers and other data to it. When you're ready to send the request, you can call the close method. This will return a Future that will resolve to an HttpClientResponse instance.

The response object provides a way to access the headers and body of the response. The body can be accessed as a stream, which makes it easy to process large responses.

Overall, Dart's HttpClient class makes it easy to make HTTP requests and process the responses. It's a great choice for use with Flutter, due to its support for streaming data.

Fetching and displaying data from APIs in Flutter

After completing this tutorial, you will be able to fetch and display data from APIs in your Flutter apps.

We'll start by creating a simple app that fetches data from the GitHub API and displays it in a ListView.

To do this, we'll use the http package.

First, add the http package to your pubspec.yaml file:

dependencies:

http: ^0.12.0+2

Next, import the package in your main.dart file:

```
import 'package:http/http.dart' as http;
```

Now we can fetch data from the GitHub API.

To do this, we'll use the http.get() method.

This method takes a URL as its first argument and returns a Future.

A Future is an asynchronous operation that returns a value in the future.

We can use the then() method to execute code when the Future completes.

The then() method takes a callback function as its argument.

This callback function takes the value returned by the Future as its argument.

In our case, the value returned by the Future will be a Response object.

The Response object has a body property that contains the data returned by the API.

We can use the jsonDecode() method to convert the data into a Map.

Finally, we can use the ListView.builder() widget to display the data in a list.

The ListView.builder() widget takes an itemCount argument which specifies the number of items to display.

It also takes an itemBuilder callback function which is called for each item.

This callback function takes two arguments: the context and the index of the item.

The context argument is used to access the theme and other resources.

The index argument is used to determine which item is being built.

Inside the itemBuilder callback function, we can return a widget for each item.

In our case, we'll return a ListTile widget.

The ListTile widget takes a title and a subtitle.

We can use the index argument to get the data for the correct item.

Now we just need to fetch the data and pass it to the ListView.builder() widget.

We can do this in the initState() method.

The initState() method is called when the widget is first created.

Inside the initState() method, we'll use the http.get() method to fetch the data.

Then we'll use the jsonDecode() method to convert the data into a Map.

Finally, we'll pass the data to the ListView.builder() widget.

Now run the app and you should see the data from the GitHub API displayed in a list.

Working with RESTful services and JSON data in Flutter

When working with RESTful services and JSON data in Flutter, it is important to understand how to fetch data from a remote server and how to decode JSON data. The process of fetching data from a remote server can be done using the http package. The http package provides a simple way to make HTTP requests and receive responses from a remote server. Once the data has been fetched from the remote server, it can be decoded using the json package. The json package provides a simple way to decode JSON data.

Authentication and secure communication in Flutter

When building apps that communicate with servers, it's important to think about security. Flutter has a few mechanisms that make it easy to securely communicate with servers.

One way to ensure secure communication is to use HTTPS. HTTPS is a protocol that encrypts communication between a client and a server. This means that if someone were to intercept the communication, they would not be able to read it.

To use HTTPS in Flutter, you can use the http package. The http package provides a convenient way to make HTTP requests. It also has support for HTTPS.

Another way to ensure secure communication is to use a VPN. A VPN is a private network that encrypts communication between a client and a server. This means that even if someone were to intercept the communication, they would not be able to read it.

To use a VPN in Flutter, you can use the flutter_vpn package. The flutter_vpn package makes it easy to connect to a VPN server. It also provides a convenient way to manage VPN connections.

Both HTTPS and VPNs are important tools for securing communication. When building apps that communicate with servers, it's important to use both HTTPS and VPNs to ensure secure communication.

Using libraries for networking (Dio, http, Chopper) in Flutter

If you're looking to network in Flutter, the first place you should look is the libraries. There are a few different libraries that can help you with networking, including Dio, http, and Chopper. Each of these libraries has its own strengths and weaknesses, so it's important to choose the one that's right for your needs.

Dio is a great choice for networking if you need a lot of flexibility. It's a powerful library that offers a wide range of features. However, it can be a bit overwhelming for beginners. If you're just starting out with Flutter, you might want to try a simpler library like http or Chopper.

http is a good choice if you need a simple way to make HTTP requests. It's a lightweight library that doesn't offer as many features as Dio, but it's much easier to use.

Chopper is a great choice if you need to make complex HTTP requests. It's a powerful library that offers a wide range of features. However, it can be a bit overwhelming for beginners. If you're just starting out with Flutter, you might want to try a simpler library like http or Dio.

Capter 6: Data Persistence and Storage in Flutter

Introduction to data persistence in Flutter

Data persistence is the act of storing data in a persistent storage medium, such as a file or database. When data is persisted, it is typically done so in a format that can be easily retrieved and used by the application. In the context of Flutter, data persistence can be used to store data that should be available to the application even after the application is closed.

There are many different ways to store data persistently in Flutter. The most common way is to use a database. Databases are powerful tools that allow applications to store and retrieve data in a structured way. Flutter provides a number of different ways to access databases, including through the use of plugins.

Another common way to store data persistently in Flutter is through the use of files. Files are a simple way to store data and can be easily accessed by the application. Flutter provides a number of different ways to read and write files, including through the use of the dart:io library.

In addition to database and file-based storage, there are a number of other ways to store data persistently in Flutter. These include shared preferences, key-value pairs, and more. Each of these has their own advantages and disadvantages, and it is up to the developer to choose the right solution for their needs.

Data persistence is a critical part of many applications. It allows data to be stored and retrieved even after the application is closed. In the context of Flutter, there are a number of different ways to achieve data persistence. The most common way is to use a database, but files and other storage solutions are also available.

Working with local databases (Sqflite, Moor) in Flutter

Android and iOS applications written in Dart can make use of a plugin called sqflite to access local databases. This plugin is based on the sqllite 3 library and provides a simple interface to query and insert data into sqlite databases.

Moor is another plugin that can be used to access local databases in Flutter. Moor is based on the active record pattern and provides a more object-oriented approach to working with data.

Both sqflite and moor can be used to persist data locally on a device. This can be useful for storing data that does not need to be synced with a remote server or for storing data that should be available offline.

To use either of these plugins, you first need to create a database file. This can be done using a tool like sqlite3 or by using the moor_cli tool. Once you have created a database file, you can then use the sqflite or moor plugin to open a connection to the database and start querying and inserting data.

Storing data in key-value pairs (SharedPreferences) in Flutter

SharedPreferences is a great way to store key-value pairs in Flutter. To use SharedPreferences, you first need to create a reference to the object. You can do this by using the getInstance() method. Once you have a reference to the SharedPreferences object, you can use the putString() method to store data. The putString() method takes two arguments, the key and the value. The key is used to identify the data, and the value is the data that you want to store.

To retrieve data from SharedPreferences, you can use the getString() method. This method takes the key as an argument and returns the data associated with that key.

SharedPreferences is a great way to store data in key-value pairs. It is easy to use and can be a great way to store data in your Flutter applications.

File storage and working with images in Flutter

In Flutter, data is stored in a number of ways. One way is through files. When working with files, it is important to understand how they are stored and accessed. In addition, working with images in Flutter is also a key part of data persistence and storage.

Files are stored in a number of places on a device. In iOS, they are stored in the Documents directory. On Android, they are stored in the app's data directory. In order to access a file, you must first get a reference to the file. This is done using the path_provider package.

Once you have a reference to the file, you can then read or write to it. Reading and writing to files is done using the File class. This class provides a number of methods for reading and writing files.

In addition to files, images are also stored in a number of ways. Images can be stored as assets or in the file system. When working with images, it is important to understand how they are stored and accessed.

Assets are stored in the asset bundle. The asset bundle is a collection of files that are packaged with the app. To access an asset, you must first get a reference to the asset. This is done using the Asset class.

Once you have a reference to the asset, you can then load the image. This is done using the Image.asset method. This method takes in the asset's path and returns an Image widget.

In order to store an image in the file system, you must first get a reference to the file. This is done using the path_provider package. Once you have a reference to the file, you can then write to it. This is done using the File class.

The File class provides a number of methods for writing to files. In order to write an image to a file, you must first convert the image to a byte array. This is done using the Image.toByteData method.

Once the image is converted to a byte array, you can then write it to the file.

Flutter provides a number of ways to store and work with data. Files and images are just two of the ways that data can be stored. In order to work with files and images, it is important to understand how they are stored and accessed.

Using cloud-based storage (Firebase Cloud Storage) in Flutter

Firebase Cloud Storage is a cloud-based object storage service from Google that lets you store and serve user-generated content, such as photos and videos.

Using Firebase Cloud Storage in Flutter is a great way to keep your app data backed up and accessible on all devices. Plus, since the service is cloud-based, your data is always available, even if your app is offline.

To use Firebase Cloud Storage in your Flutter app, you first need to create a Firebase project and enable the Cloud Storage API. Then, you can use the Firebase Storage package to access the service.

Here's a quick example of how to use Firebase Cloud Storage in Flutter:

```dart
import
'package:firebase_storage/firebase_storage.dart';

void main() {

final storage = FirebaseStorage.instance;

// Upload a file

final String filePath = 'path/to/file.txt';

final StorageReference storageRef =
storage.ref().child(filePath);

final StorageUploadTask uploadTask =
storageRef.putFile(

File(filePath),

);

// Download a file

final StorageReference downloadRef =
storage.ref().child(filePath);

final StorageFileDownloadTask downloadTask =
downloadRef.writeToFile(

File(filePath),
```

```
);

}
```

Chapter 7: Working with External APIs and Services in Flutter

Integrating Firebase services (Authentication, Firestore, Cloud Messaging) in Flutter

When it comes to building Flutter apps, there are a lot of different options when it comes to external APIs and services. One popular option is Firebase, which offers a number of different services that can be easily integrated into Flutter apps.

One of the most popular Firebase services is Authentication, which allows users to sign in to your app using their Google or Facebook account. This makes it easy for users to get started with your app, and it also helps to keep your app secure.

Another popular Firebase service is Firestore, which is a cloud-based database that makes it easy to store and sync data across devices. This is a great option for apps that need to keep data in sync across multiple devices, or for apps that need to store a lot of data.

Finally, Firebase also offers Cloud Messaging, which allows you to send push notifications to users of your app. This is a great way to keep users up-to-date on new features or changes to your app, and it can also be used to send promotional messages or other important information.

Integrating these Firebase services into your Flutter app is easy, and there are a number of different tutorials and guides available online. Once you have your app set up with Firebase, you'll be able to take advantage of all of these great features, and more.

Using device features (Camera, Location, Sensors) in Flutter

When it comes to using device features in Flutter, there are a few different ways to go about it. One option is to use the built-in APIs that are provided by the operating system, such as the Camera or Location API. Another option is to use third-party services, such as the Google Maps API.

If you want to use the built-in APIs, you'll need to use the plugin system in Flutter. This is because the built-in APIs are not part of the core Flutter framework. To use a plugin, you first need to add it to your pubspec.yaml file. For example, to use the Camera API, you would add the camera plugin to your pubspec.yaml file.

Once the plugin is added to your pubspec.yaml file, you can import it into your Dart code and use it. For example, to take a picture with the Camera API, you would use the following code:

```
import 'package:camera/camera.dart';

Future<void> takePicture() async {

final cameras = await availableCameras();

final firstCamera = cameras.first;

final result = await takePicture(firstCamera);

}
```

If you want to use third-party services, you'll need to create an account and obtain an API key. Once you have an API key, you can use it to access the services. For example, to use the Google Maps API, you would use the following code:

```dart
import
'package:google_maps_flutter/google_maps_flutter
.dart';

Future<void> showMap() async {

final apiKey = 'YOUR_API_KEY';

final GoogleMapController controller = await
getMapController(apiKey);

controller.showMarker(MarkerOptions(

position: LatLng(37.4219999, -122.0840575),

infoWindowText: InfoWindowText('Google HQ',
'1600 Amphitheatre Pkwy'),

));

}
```

Accessing device contacts and calendar events in Flutter

When it comes to working with external APIs and services in Flutter, one of the most important things you can do is access device contacts and calendar events. This can be a great way to keep track of your schedule and make sure you're always in touch with the people you need to be.

In order to access contacts and calendar events in Flutter, you'll need to use the following plugins:

- [path_provider](https://pub.dev/packages/path_provider)
- [device_calendar](https://pub.dev/packages/device_calendar)
- [contacts_service](https://pub.dev/packages/contacts_service)

Once you have these plugins installed, you can start by using the `path_provider` plugin to get the path to the directory where your contacts and calendar events are stored. Then, you can use the `device_calendar` and `contacts_service` plugins to access the contacts and calendar events respectively.

Here's a quick example of how you might use these plugins to access your device's contacts and calendar events:

```dart
import 'dart:io';
```

```dart
import
'package:path_provider/path_provider.dart';

import
'package:device_calendar/device_calendar.dart';

import
'package:contacts_service/contacts_service.dart';

// Get the path to the directory where contacts
and calendar events are stored

Future<String> get _localPath async {

final directory = await
getApplicationDocumentsDirectory();

return directory.path;

}

// Get a reference to the device's contacts

Future<Iterable<Contact>> get _contacts async {

// Get the path to the contacts directory

final path = await _localPath;

// Read the contacts from the directory

final contacts = await
ContactsService.getContacts(path);

// Return the contacts
```

```
  return contacts;

}

// Get a reference to the device's calendar events

Future<Iterable<Event>> get _events async {

// Get the path to the calendar events directory

final path = await _localPath;

// Read the calendar events from the directory

final events = await
DeviceCalendar.getEvents(path);

// Return the calendar events

return events;

}
```
```

As you can see, accessing contacts and calendar events in Flutter is a pretty straightforward process. By using the plugins mentioned above, you can easily get a reference to both the contacts and calendar events stored on your device.
```

Push notifications and in-app messaging in Flutter

Push notifications and in-app messaging are two important ways to keep your users engaged with your app. In Flutter, there are a few different ways to handle push notifications and in-app messaging.

One way to handle push notifications is to use the Firebase Cloud Messaging service. With Firebase Cloud Messaging, you can send push notifications to your users without having to write any code. All you need to do is create a Firebase project, add the Firebase Cloud Messaging SDK to your app, and then configure your app to receive push notifications.

Another way to handle push notifications is to use the local_notifications plugin. This plugin allows you to schedule and display notifications within your Flutter app. The local_notifications plugin is great for displaying notifications when a user completes an action within your app, such as completing a task or level in a game.

In-app messaging is another way to keep your users engaged with your app. In-app messaging allows you to send messages to your users while they are using your app. In-app messages can be used to promote new features, give updates on app changes, or just send a message to your users.

In Flutter, there are a few different ways to handle in-app messaging. One way to handle in-app messaging is to use the Firebase Cloud Messaging service. With Firebase Cloud Messaging, you can send in-app messages to your users without having to write any code. All you need to do is create a Firebase project, add the Firebase Cloud Messaging SDK to your app, and then configure your app to receive in-app messages.

Another way to handle in-app messaging is to use the local_notifications plugin. This plugin allows you to schedule and display notifications within your Flutter app. The local_notifications plugin is great for displaying in-app messages when a user completes an action within your app, such as completing a task or level in a game.

push_notifications and in_app_messaging are two important ways to keep your users engaged with your app. In Flutter, there are a few different ways to handle push notifications and in-app messaging. With Firebase Cloud Messaging and the local_notifications plugin, you can easily add push notifications and in-app messages to your Flutter app.

Using third-party APIs (Maps, Social media, Payment gateways) in Flutter

When it comes to using third-party APIs in Flutter, there are a few things to keep in mind. First and foremost, make sure that the API you are using is compatible with Flutter. There are a few ways to do this, but the easiest way is to check the Flutter website for a list of compatible APIs.

Once you've found an API that you want to use, the next step is to figure out how to integrate it into your Flutter app. There are a few different ways to do this, but the most common way is to use a package that wraps the API for you. This way, you don't have to worry about the details of how the API works, and you can just focus on using it in your app.

There are a few things to keep in mind when using a package like this. First, make sure that you read the documentation carefully. This will help you understand how to use the package and what its capabilities are. Second, make sure to test the package thoroughly before using it in your production app. This way, you can be sure that it works as expected and that there are no unforeseen problems.

Once you've got the package set up and working in your app, you can start using the API. This will vary depending on the API, but most likely you'll be able to make calls to the API from your code and then use the data that it returns. For example, if you're using the Maps API, you can call the various methods to get information about a particular location.

As you can see, using third-party APIs in Flutter is relatively easy. Just make sure that you take the time to find a compatible API and then use a package to help you integrate it into your app. With a little bit of effort, you can add some great features to your app that would otherwise be unavailable.

Chapter 8: Flutter UI Customization and Theming

Customizing widget appearance with properties in Flutter

One of the great things about Flutter is the ability to customize the appearance of your widgets to match the look and feel of your app. In this chapter, we'll explore some of the ways you can do this by using properties like color, padding, and margin.

Color

The color property allows you to set the color of a widget. This can be useful for making a button stand out or for giving text a different color.

Padding

Padding is the space between a widget and its surroundings. You can use padding to make a widget larger or smaller.

Margin

Margin is the space between a widget and other widgets. You can use margin to create space between widgets.

Using themes for consistent app styling in Flutter

While building apps in Flutter, it is important to maintain a consistent theme throughout the app. This can be accomplished by using themes. A theme is a set of colors, text styles, and shapes that can be applied to an app.

There are two ways to create a theme:

1) Create a new ThemeData object and pass it to the MaterialApp widget.

2) Use the ThemeData.copyWith() method to create a new ThemeData object based on an existing one.

Once a theme has been created, it can be applied to an app by passing it to the MaterialApp widget.

Flutter provides a number of predefined themes that can be used as is or customized to meet the needs of your app. In addition, the ThemeData class provides a number of methods for creating new themes based on existing ones.

When using themes, it is important to keep in mind that each widget in Flutter has its own theme. This means that if you want to maintain a consistent theme throughout your app, you will need to set the theme for each widget that you create.

The best way to do this is to create a custom widget that extends the desired widget and sets the theme in its build() method. This will ensure that all of the child widgets inherit the correct theme.

For example, let's say you want to create a custom button widget that always uses the primary color from the app's theme. You would first create a class that extends the Button widget:

```
class MyButton extends Button {

@override

Widget build(BuildContext context) {

return new Theme(
```

```
data: Theme.of(context).copyWith(

buttonColor: Theme.of(context).primaryColor,

),

child: super.build(context),

);

}

}
```

Now, whenever you create a MyButton widget, it will use the primary color from the app's theme.

Themes are a powerful tool for creating consistent app styling in Flutter. By creating custom widgets that extend the standard widgets and setting the theme in the build() method, you can ensure that all of the child widgets inherit the correct theme. This will help you create apps that have a consistent look and feel.

Creating custom themes and styles in Flutter

Flutter UI Customization and Theming is a process of making your app's user interface look unique and stylized. It can be done by creating custom themes and styles for your app. This will make your app's user interface more attractive and user-friendly.

Creating custom themes and styles is not a difficult task. You just need to have a good understanding of the Flutter platform and its capabilities. Once you have a good understanding of Flutter, it will be easy for you to create custom themes and styles.

There are two ways to create custom themes and styles in Flutter. One way is to use the built-in Material Design Widgets, and the other way is to use theCupertino Widgets.

If you want to create a custom theme for your app, you need to first create a class that extends the MaterialApp class. Then, you need to override the theme property and set it to your custom theme.

If you want to create a custom style for your app, you need to create a class that extends the Style class. Then, you need to override the style property and set it to your custom style.

Once you have created your custom theme or style, you can apply it to your app by using the following code:

```
MaterialApp( title: 'My App', theme: MyCustomTheme(), home: MyHomePage(), );

CupertinoApp( title: 'My App', theme: MyCustomTheme(), home: MyHomePage(), );
```

After you have applied your custom theme or style, your app's user interface will look more attractive and user-friendly.

Working with fonts and typography in Flutter

When it comes to working with fonts and typography in Flutter, there are a few things to keep in mind. First and foremost, Flutter uses the Google Fonts library, which means that you have access to a wide variety of fonts to choose from. However, you'll need to be sure to import the font into your project before you can use it.

Once you have the font imported, you can start using it in your Flutter app. To do so, simply specify the font family when creating a new Text widget. For example, if you wanted to use the "Roboto" font, you would do so like this:

Text('Some text', style: TextStyle(fontFamily: 'Roboto')

Of course, you're not limited to just using the Google Fonts library. If you have a custom font that you want to use in your Flutter app, you can simply specify the path to the font file when creating the TextStyle object. For example, if your custom font was located in the "assets/fonts" directory, you would specify it like this:

Text('Some text', style: TextStyle(fontFamily: 'CustomFont', fontFile: 'assets/fonts/CustomFont.ttf')

And that's all there is to using fonts and typography in Flutter! With the vast array of fonts available through the Google Fonts library, and the ability to use custom fonts, you should have no trouble creating beautiful and stylish text for your Flutter app.

Animations and transitions in Flutter

Animations and transitions are an integral part of Flutter UI customization and theming. By default, Flutter provides a set of predefined and Material-based animations and transitions that can be used to enhance the user experience. However, for more customized and complex animations and transitions, developers can use the animation controller and tween classes.

The animation controller is responsible for driving the animations, while the tween class defines the animation by specifying the start and end values. In order to create a custom animation, developers need to first create an animation controller and then create a tween that defines the animation. Once the animation controller and tween are created, developers can then use the animate() method to trigger the animation.

There are a variety of ways to customize the animation and transition experience in Flutter. By using the right combination of animation controller, tween, and animate() method, developers can create custom animations and transitions that are both visually appealing and user-friendly.

Chapter 9: Advanced Flutter Concepts

Flutter's rendering and layout pipeline

Flutter's rendering and layout pipeline is a bit more complicated than one might think. In order to understand it, one must first understand the basics of how Flutter works.

Flutter is a cross-platform framework that allows developers to create native apps for both Android and iOS. Flutter uses the Dart programming language, which is compiled to native code for each platform.

Flutter apps are composed of widgets, which are self-contained units of UI. Widgets can be nested, and they can contain other widgets.

The layout of a Flutter app is done in two stages:

1. The initial layout is done when the app is first created. This is when the widgets are first laid out on the screen.

2. The second layout is done when the app is rendered. This is when the widgets are actually drawn on the screen.

The initial layout is done using a layout algorithm, which is a set of rules that determine how the widgets should be laid out on the screen. The layout algorithm is different for each platform (Android and iOS), but the basics are the same.

The second layout is done using a rendering algorithm, which is a set of rules that determine how the widgets should be drawn on the screen. The rendering algorithm is different for each platform (Android and iOS), but the basics are the same.

The layout and rendering algorithms are both executed on the UI thread.

The layout algorithm is executed first, and it determines the positions of the widgets on the screen. The rendering algorithm is executed second, and it draws the widgets on the screen.

Performance optimization techniques in Flutter

Flutter is a mobile app SDK that allows you to build high-quality native apps for iOS and Android. One of the key features of Flutter is its high-performance graphics engine, which allows you to create beautiful user interfaces.

However, as with any tool, there are always ways to optimize its performance. In this chapter, we'll explore some of the techniques you can use to optimize the performance of your Flutter apps.

One of the first things you can do to optimize performance is to use the latest stable version of Flutter. The Flutter team is constantly working to improve performance, so upgrading to the latest version can give you a significant boost.

Another way to improve performance is to use the release mode when compiling your app. Release mode enables all the optimizations that the Dart compiler can perform, and it also disables asserts and debug print statements. This can give you a significant performance boost, especially on release builds.

If you're using any third-party libraries, it's also worth checking to see if there are any performance optimizations that you can make. For example, the Flutter team has recently released an optimized version of the popular Firebase library.

Finally, if you're still having performance issues, it's worth considering using profile mode. Profile mode allows you to see exactly where your app is spending its time, which can be invaluable for pinpointing performance bottlenecks.

By following these tips, you can make sure that your Flutter apps are running at peak performance.

Internationalization and localization in Flutter

Flutter is an open-source mobile application development framework created by Google. It is used to develop applications for Android and iOS. Flutter is also used to develop web and desktop applications.

Flutter has a number of features that make it well suited for developing internationalized and localized applications. First, Flutter uses the Unicode standard for its characters, which includes support for a wide range of languages. Second, Flutter's text rendering engine supports a number of internationalized features, such as complex text layout, bidirectional text, and text scaling. Third, Flutter provides a set of internationalization and localization APIs that make it easy to develop applications that support multiple languages.

Fourth, Flutter includes a number of tools that can be used to test internationalized and localized applications. These tools can be used to test the application's user interface, text rendering, and internationalization and localization APIs.

fifth, Flutter's developer community is active and growing, and there are a number of resources available to help developers with internationalization and localization.

In conclusion, Flutter is a good choice for developing internationalized and localized applications. Flutter's support for a wide range of languages, its text rendering engine, and its internationalization and localization APIs make it an ideal platform for developing such applications.

Accessibility considerations and best practices in Flutter

Flutter is a mobile app SDK that allows you to develop high-quality native apps for iOS and Android. One of the key advantages of Flutter is its ability to provide excellent accessibility support for both platforms.

In order to ensure that your Flutter app is accessible to as many users as possible, there are a few considerations and best practices to keep in mind.

First, when developing your app, be sure to test it with a variety of accessibility tools and services. This will help you identify any potential accessibility issues so that you can address them before your app is released.

Second, Flutter provides a number of built-in accessibility features, such as support for screen readers and text-to-speech. Be sure to take advantage of these features to make your app as accessible as possible.

Finally, keep in mind that accessibility is an ongoing process. As new accessibility technologies and standards emerge, be sure to update your app accordingly. By following these simple guidelines, you can ensure that your Flutter app is accessible to everyone.

Testing and debugging Flutter applications

Testing and debugging Flutter applications can be challenging, but there are a few tools and techniques that can make the process easier. The first step is to identify the problem. Once the problem is identified, it is important to understand the code and the application architecture. This will help you determine the best way to fix the problem.

There are a few different ways to test and debug Flutter applications. The most common way is to use the flutter_test package. This package provides a number of tools and utilities for testing and debugging Flutter applications. The flutter_driver package is also a great tool for testing and debugging Flutter applications. This package allows you to run your Flutter application on a device or simulator and interact with it using a set of APIs.

Once you have identified the problem, the next step is to fix the problem. This can be done by modifying the code or by using a different tool or technique. If the problem is with the code, it is important to understand the code and the application architecture. This will help you determine the best way to fix the problem. If the problem is with a tool or technique, it is important to find a replacement that works better.

After the problem is fixed, it is important to test the fix. This can be done by running the application on a device or simulator and testing it. If the fix works, it is important to commit the fix to the codebase. This will help other developers who are working on the same codebase.

Chapter 10: Flutter and Native Device Features

Integrating Flutter with existing native code (Android and iOS)

If you're looking to add Flutter to an existing app written in Java or Objective-C, you can do so by creating a new Flutter module. This module will house all of your Flutter code, and you can then reference it from your existing codebase.

To integrate Flutter with native code, you'll first need to add the Flutter module to your project. This can be done using the flutter create command, or by adding it to your pubspec.yaml file.

Once the module is added, you can then start referencing it from your existing code. For example, if you have a button in your app that you want to be a Flutter button, you can add the following code to your view controller:

```
import 'package:flutter/widgets.dart';

...

FlatButton(
```

```
child: Text('Flutter button'),

onPressed: () {

// Do something here

},

)
```

This will render a button that looks and feels like a Flutter button, but is actually being controlled by your existing code.

You can also access other native features from your Flutter code. For example, if you want to use the device's camera, you can do so by using the camera plugin:

```
import 'package:camera/camera.dart';

...

CameraController camera;

...

camera = CameraController(cameras[0],
ResolutionPreset.medium);
```

```
camera.initialize().then((_) {

if (!mounted) {

return;

}

setState(() {});

});
```

This will give you access to the device's camera, and you can then use it to take pictures or videos.

Integrating Flutter with existing native code can be a great way to add new features to your app without having to rewrite your entire codebase. By using the tools and plugins available, you can easily add Flutter to your existing app and take advantage of all the benefits it has to offer.

Using platform channels for bi-directional communication in Flutter

In Flutter, platform channels are used for bi-directional communication between the Flutter framework and native platform code. This communication is used to provide access to platform-specific features, such as accessing the device camera.

In order to use platform channels, the first step is to create a channel. This is done by passing a name and an optional set of codecs to the MethodChannel constructor. The name of the channel must be unique across all channels in the application. Once the channel is created, it can be used to invoke platform-specific code.

To invoke platform-specific code, the invokeMethod method is used. This method takes a method name and optional set of arguments. The method name is used to identify the platform-specific code that should be executed. The optional set of arguments is used to pass data to the platform-specific code.

After the platform-specific code is executed, the results are returned through a Future. This Future is passed to the invokeMethod call as the second argument. The platform-specific code can also return an error through this Future.

In order to receive data from the platform-specific code, the setMethodCallHandler method is used. This method takes a callback that is invoked when the platform-specific code invokes a method on the channel. The callback takes a MethodCall instance as an argument. This instance can be used to get the name of the invoked method and the arguments passed to it.

Platform channels provide a powerful way to add platform-specific functionality to a Flutter application. They also provide a way for the platform-specific code to communicate back to the Flutter code. This communication is used to provide a responsive user experience.

Accessing device features and sensors in Flutter

Flutter provides a set of widgets that gives you access to all the native device features and sensors on your mobile device. These widgets are available in the flutter_native_feature package.

To use the flutter_native_feature package, you first need to add it to your pubspec.yaml file:

dependencies:

flutter_native_feature: "^0.1.0"

Then, you can use the widgets in your code:

```dart
import
'package:flutter_native_feature/flutter_native_feat
ure.dart';

// Access the camera

var camera = new Camera();

// Access the accelerometer

var accelerometer = new Accelerometer();

// Access the gyroscope

var gyroscope = new Gyroscope();

// Access the light sensor

var light = new Light();

// Access the pressure sensor

var pressure = new Pressure();

// Access the proximity sensor

var proximity = new Proximity();

// Access the temperature sensor

var temperature = new Temperature();
```

Working with native APIs and libraries in Flutter

Flutter is an amazing tool for creating cross-platform applications with a single codebase. But sometimes, you need the power of a native API or library to get the job done.

Working with native APIs and libraries in Flutter is easy and straightforward. All you need to do is import the relevant package, and you're good to go.

For example, let's say you want to use the camera API to take a photo. First, you would import the camera package:

```
import 'package:camera/camera.dart';
```

Then, you can use the camera API to take a photo:

```
CameraController controller = CameraController(camera);

controller.takePicture();
```

It's that easy! You can use any native API or library in Flutter with just a few lines of code.

Building custom Flutter plugins

Flutter is a great platform for building custom plugins that can be used to access native device features. In this chapter, we'll cover how to build a custom plugin that can be used to access the camera on a device. We'll also cover how to use the plugin within a Flutter app.

Building the plugin will require some knowledge of the native platform (iOS or Android) that the plugin will be used on. For this example, we'll be building a plugin for iOS.

The first step is to create a new class that extends the AbstractMethodChannel class. This class will be used to communicate with the native platform.

Next, we need to override the invokeMethod() method. This method will be called whenever the plugin is invoked from a Flutter app. Within this method, we'll check the method being invoked and call the appropriate native method.

For this example, we'll only be implementing a single method, takePicture(). This method will take a picture using the device's camera and return the path to the saved image.

Once the plugin class is implemented, we need to register it with the Flutter platform. This is done by adding a static method that returns an instance of the plugin class.

With the plugin class implemented and registered, we can now use it within a Flutter app.

To use the plugin, we first need to import it. Then, we can create a new instance of the plugin class and invoke the takePicture() method. This method will return a Future that will resolve to the path of the saved image.

Building custom Flutter plugins is a great way to access native device features from within a Flutter app. By using the invokeMethod() method, we can easily call native methods and receive data back from them. This makes it possible to build powerful plugins that can greatly extend the capabilities of a Flutter app.

Chapter 11: Flutter and Web Development

Introduction to Flutter web development

Flutter is a cross-platform mobile app development framework created by Google. It allows developers to create native-looking Android and iOS apps from a single codebase. Flutter apps are written in the Dart programming language and make use of the Flutter framework, which includes a number of libraries and tools for creating user interfaces, managing app state, and more.

Flutter web development is still in its early stages, but it's already possible to create web apps that look and feel like native apps. The biggest advantage of using Flutter for web development is that you can reuse your existing Dart code and libraries. This means that you can get started with Flutter web development without having to learn a new language or framework.

One of the most important aspects of creating a successful web app is choosing the right hosting platform. There are a number of options available, but the two most popular are Firebase and

Heroku. Firebase is a Google-owned platform that offers a number of features for Flutter web apps, including hosting, database, and authentication. Heroku is a popular platform-as-a-service that offers an easy way to deploy and scale Flutter web apps.

When it comes to choosing a domain name for your app, there are a few things to keep in mind. First, try to choose a .com domain name that's short and easy to remember. Second, avoid using hyphens or numbers in your domain name. And third, make sure your domain name is relevant to your app's content.

Once you've chosen a hosting platform and domain name, you're ready to start building your Flutter web app. The first thing you'll need to do is install the Flutter SDK. Then, you can create a new Flutter project using the command line or your favorite text editor.

Once you have a Flutter project set up, you can start adding features to your app. For example, you can add a login page, a home page, and a settings page. You can also add support for push notifications and in-app purchases.

Flutter web development is still in its early stages, but it's already possible to create web apps that look and feel like native apps. The biggest advantage of using Flutter for web development is that you can reuse your existing Dart code and libraries. This means that you can get started with Flutter web development without having to learn a new language or framework.

Building responsive web interfaces with Flutter

In the past, web development has been limited to building static web pages. However, with the advent of technologies like Flutter, web developers can now create responsive web interfaces that look and feel just like native mobile apps.

Flutter is a mobile UI framework that allows developers to create high-quality, responsive user interfaces for both iOS and Android. With Flutter, developers can create a single codebase that can be compiled to native code for both platforms. This means that developers can create one set of code that will work on both iOS and Android devices.

Flutter's responsive UI is based on a set of Widgets that can be used to build up complex user interfaces. These Widgets are designed to be easy to use and to be highly customizable. This makes it easy for developers to create responsive user interfaces that look and feel great on all devices.

In addition to being responsive, Flutter's Widgets are also very fast. This is because they are compiled to native code. This means that they can take advantage of all the performance benefits that come with native code.

Overall, Flutter is a great tool for web developers who want to create responsive user interfaces. With Flutter, developers can create high-quality, responsive user interfaces that look and feel just like native mobile apps.

Navigation and routing in Flutter web

Flutter web provides a great way to navigate and route around your web app. In this chapter, we'll learn how to use the Navigator and Route classes to manage our app's navigation.

The Navigator class is used to manage the stack of routes in our app. We can push and pop routes to add or remove pages from our app. The Route class represents a single page in our app.

To use the Navigator, we first need to create a MaterialApp. The MaterialApp widget is used to initialize the navigator. We can then use the navigator's push and pop methods to add and remove routes from the stack.

The push method takes a Route object as its argument. The Route class represents a single page in our app. We can create a Route by subclassing the MaterialPageRoute class.

The MaterialPageRoute class provides a number of features that we can use to customize our route. For example, we can specify the page's title, and we can also specify a custom transitions to use when the route is pushed or popped.

In addition to the Navigator and Route classes, the flutter_web package also provides a number of other classes that can be used to manage our app's navigation. For example, we can use the History class to keep track of the routes that have been pushed onto the stack.

The flutter_web package also provides a number of utility functions that can be used to make working with the Navigator and Route classes easier. For example, the Navigator.of() function can be used to get a reference to the current navigator.

Overall, the Navigator and Route classes provide a great way to manage our app's navigation. They give us a lot of flexibility in how we want to

structure our app, and they make it easy to add
and remove pages.

Interacting with web APIs and services in Flutter

In this chapter, we'll learn how to interact with
web APIs and services in Flutter. We'll start by
creating a simple app that fetches data from a
public API and displays it in a ListView. Then, we'll
add the ability to save data locally using SQlite.
Finally, we'll add the ability to upload data to a
server.

Creating the app is simple and only requires a few
steps. First, create a new Flutter application and
add the following dependencies to your
pubspec.yaml file:

http: ^0.12.0+2 sqflite: ^1.1.6

Then, create a new file called api_provider.dart
and add the following code:

```dart
import 'dart:convert'; import
'package:http/http.dart' as http; class ApiProvider
{ final String _baseUrl =
"https://jsonplaceholder.typicode.com";
Future<List<dynamic>> getPosts() async { final
response = await http.get("$_baseUrl/posts"); if
(response.statusCode == 200) { return
json.decode(response.body); } else { throw
Exception("Failed to load posts"); } } }
```

This code defines a simple ApiProvider class that
makes a GET request to the JSONPlaceholder API.
The data is then parsed into a List of dynamic
objects.

To use the ApiProvider, add the following code to
your main.dart file:

```dart
import 'package:flutter/material.dart'; import
'package:flutter_app/api_provider.dart'; void
main() => runApp(MyApp()); class MyApp extends
StatelessWidget { @override Widget
build(BuildContext context) { return MaterialApp(
title: 'Flutter and Web API', theme: ThemeData(
primarySwatch: Colors.blue, ), home:
MyHomePage(), ); } } class MyHomePage extends
```

```
StatelessWidget { final ApiProvider _apiProvider =
ApiProvider(); @override Widget
build(BuildContext context) { return Scaffold(
appBar: AppBar( title: Text("Flutter and Web
API"), ), body: Center( child: FutureBuilder( future:
_apiProvider.getPosts(), builder: (BuildContext
context, AsyncSnapshot snapshot) { if
(snapshot.connectionState ==
ConnectionState.done) { if (snapshot.hasError) {
return Text("Failed to load data"); } else { return
ListView.builder( itemCount: snapshot.data.length,
itemBuilder: (BuildContext context, int index) {
return ListTile( title:
Text(snapshot.data[index]["title"]), subtitle:
Text(snapshot.data[index]["body"]), ); }, ); } } else {
return CircularProgressIndicator(); } }, ), ), ); } }
```

In this code, we first create an instance of the
ApiProvider. We then use the FutureBuilder
widget to make a GET request to the
JSONPlaceholder API. The data is then displayed in
a ListView.

If we run the app now, we should see a list of posts
from the JSONPlaceholder API.

As Flutter continues to grow in popularity, more and more developers are looking into how to deploy Flutter web applications. There are a few different ways to do this, and the best method may vary depending on your specific needs.

One popular way to deploy Flutter web apps is using the Google App Engine. The App Engine is a flexible platform that can host a variety of different types of applications. It's easy to set up and get started with, and it provides a lot of flexibility in terms of scaling and managing your app.

Another popular option for deploying Flutter web apps is using Firebase. Firebase is a powerful platform that provides a lot of features for building and managing web applications. It's easy to use and get started with, and it offers a lot of flexibility in terms of how you deploy and manage your app.

No matter which method you choose, deploying a Flutter web app is a fairly straightforward process. In most cases, you'll just need to build your app using the flutter build command, and then deploy it using the chosen platform's tools.

If you're looking to deploy a Flutter web app, there are a few different options to choose from. The best method may vary depending on your specific needs, but in most cases, the process is fairly straightforward.

Chapter 12: Deploying and Publishing Flutter Apps

Building and generating app bundles and APKs (Android) in Flutter

Building and generating app bundles and APKs (Android) in Flutter is a process that is related to deploying and publishing Flutter apps. This process allows you to build your app for release, generate an app bundle or APK, and then publish your app to an app store.

Building for release

When you are ready to release your app, you will need to build it for release. This can be done by running the flutter build command with the -- release flag. This will generate a release build of your app.

Generating an app bundle or APK

Once you have a release build of your app, you can generate an app bundle or APK. An app bundle is a package of your app that can be deployed to an app store. An APK is a single file that can be deployed to an Android device.

To generate an app bundle, you can use the flutter build appbundle command. This will generate a file called app-release.aab in the build/app/outputs/bundle/release/ directory.

To generate an APK, you can use the flutter build apk command. This will generate a file called app-release.apk in the build/app/outputs/apk/release/ directory.

Publishing your app

Once you have generated an app bundle or APK, you can publish your app to an app store. For Android, you can publish your app to the Google Play Store. For iOS, you can publish your app to the App Store.

Archiving and distributing apps on the App Store (iOS)

The process for archiving and distributing apps on the App Store is relatively simple and straightforward. After creating an app in Xcode, developers can simply go to the Product menu and select Archive. This will generate a signed and packaged version of the app that is ready to be submitted to the App Store.

Once the app is submitted, it will go through a review process by Apple. Once it is approved, it will be made available on the App Store for download.

Creating app icons and launch screens for Flutter Apps

Creating app icons and launch screens for Flutter Apps is a simple process that just requires a few steps. First, create a new folder in your project called "icons" and add your app icon to it. Next, open the pubspec.yaml file and add the following lines to the flutter section:

assets: - icons/<your-icon-filename>

Finally, run flutter pub get on the command line to fetch the new icon.

Now that you have your app icon, you need to create a launch screen. The launch screen is the first thing users will see when they open your app, so it's important to make a good impression.

To create a launch screen, simply create a new file called "launch_screen.dart" in your project and add the following code to it:

```
import 'package:flutter/material.dart'; class
LaunchScreen extends StatelessWidget {
@override Widget build(BuildContext context) {
return Scaffold( body: Center( child:
Image.asset('icons/<your-icon-filename>'), ), ); } }
```

Now, when you run your app, the launch screen will be displayed before your app loads.

Testing and debugging Flutter Apps for release

When you are ready to release your Flutter app to the world, you need to make sure it is properly tested and debugged. Otherwise, you may find yourself with a lot of unhappy users!

There are a few different ways to test and debug Flutter apps. The first is to use the built-in tools in the IDE, such as the debugger and console. These can be very helpful in finding and fixing bugs.

Another way to test and debug Flutter apps is to use third-party tools. These can be either paid or free, and they offer a variety of features that can help you find and fix bugs.

Finally, you can also use physical devices to test and debug your Flutter app. This is often the best way to test how your app will work on different types of devices.

Whichever method you choose, make sure to thoroughly test your app before releasing it to the public. A little bit of testing and debugging now can save you a lot of headaches later!

Publishing Flutter apps to Google Play Store and App Store

After you've built your Flutter app, it's time to deploy it to the Google Play Store and App Store.

This process is relatively simple, but there are a few things to keep in mind.

First, you'll need to create a developer account with each store. This process is free, but you will need to provide some personal information and credit card details. Once you've created your accounts, you can log in and begin the process of submitting your app.

The first thing you'll need to do is provide some basic information about your app, including its name, description, and category. You'll also need to upload your app's binary file. This is the file that contains your app's code and assets.

Once you've submitted this information, you'll need to wait for your app to be reviewed by the store's staff. This process can take a few days, but once your app is approved, it will be available for download by users.

Congratulations! By following these steps, you've successfully published your Flutter app to the Google Play Store and App Store.

（